UNDERSTANDING WORKPLACE BULLYING

UNDERSTANDING WORKPLACE BULLYING

LINDA SUE MATA

Book Vine Press
2516 Highland Dr.
Palatine, IL 60067

Contents

Introduction

The significance of studying "workplace bullying" or "workplace mobbing" stems from the urgent need to curb this silent epidemic that is sweeping through the workplace (Canadian Safety Council, 2004). Given its prevalence and far reaching implications, a growing awareness of bullying is required. Not only is it costly to victims and their families and communities, but it creates an unhealthy workplace, detrimental to the organization and society as well (Leyman, 1992). According to the European Agency for Safety and Health at Work, there is no single definition of "Workplace Bullying" that has been agreed upon internationally. It has been defined as "repeated, unreasonable behavior directed towards an employee or a group of employees that creates a risk to health and safety (Hoel & Cooper, 2000). Unreasonable behavior has been defined as behavior that a reasonable person having regard to all the circumstances, would expect to victimize, humiliate, undermine or threaten. It includes actions of an individual or a group. "Risk to health and safety" includes risk to the mental and physical health of an employee.

There are many sources that now recognize the severe and urgent problems resulting from workplace bullying, but many more are needed. Bullying is not a new practice and has been used as a management tool for many years. It continues, at least partly, because it seems to work (Paice & Firth-Cozers, 2003).

In recent decades, bullying has come to be realized as a problem that is ultimately counterproductive. It is now a recognized problem and a cause of major concern. Victims stand to lose their self-esteem, their health, and even their careers (Peyton, 2003). Extensive research has been conducted and the findings are clearly conclusive in defining workplace bullying as a leading cause of stress, illness, and post—traumatic stress disorder. It is also escalating in workplaces throughout the world and in the US, and at least one of every six workers has experienced bullying.

In 2001, a report published under the auspices of the Health and Safety Authority (HSA) found that bullying may account for serious health problems for those who have been bullied, and also affects those who are mere bystanders. Bullying also leads to low productivity in the organization (Rathery, 2005). A 1999 report of the International Labor Organization (ILO), found bullying to be one of the most serious problems facing the workplace in the "New Millennium". Workplace bullying or mobbing is usually displayed as indirect aggression. Indirect aggression is unclear and more studies are needed to produce information about indirect aggression in adults. One problem is most studies focus on physical aggression and workplace bullying is generally psychological.

Studies suggest that rudeness resulting from bullying and incivility affect job satisfaction, self-esteem, and ultimately job performance. Self-esteem is how one perceives himself often in response to how he or she feels perceived by others. Rudeness is insensitive or disrespectful behavior enacted by a person that displays a lack of regard for others (Erez & Porath, 2007). Studies find rudeness reduces performance on both routine tasks and creative tasks and also decreases helpfulness (Erez & Porath, 2007).

Erez and Porath (2007) identify three types of rudeness: rudeness instigated by a direct authority figure, rudeness delivered by a third party, and imagined rudeness. Several researchers have found that rude behaviors are linked to employee's retaliatory behaviors (Bris, Tripp & Kramer, 1997; Skarlucki & Folger, 1997) counterproductive behaviors (Duffy, Ganster, & Pagon, 2002), and withdrawal of leader support (Tyler & Blader, 2000). Recent studies suggest that targets of rudeness report psychological distress (Cortina, Magley, Williams et Langhart, 2001), and negative emotional effects (Peason & Porath, 2005). Negative emotions and attitudes may in turn affect individual's functioning and performance in a variety of ways (Ellis, Moore, Varner, & Ottaway, 1997; Ellis, Varner, Bono & Patton, 2001).

This book suggests ways organizational culture and leadership may contribute to bullying. Workplace bullying generally occurs where social climates in the workplace lead to harsh personalized conflict or even 'office wars' and the objective becomes to ultimately destroy the opponent (Van de Vliet, 1998). Organizations tolerating such incivility and rudeness send a signal throughout the organization that escalates into conflict (Namie, 2002, 2003).

This social climate arises from the organization's culture that consists of the assumptions, values, and norms of the organization's members. It is crucial for leadership to assume roles appropriate to prevent bullying from escalating and reaching magnitudes of uncontrollable proportions. More studies and empirical data are needed to identify ways to combat bullying and incivility in the workplace. A review of the literature on workplace bullying suggests there needs to be more training of employees in the organization at all levels to confront this issue, and more legislation needs to be enacted to enforce laws outlawing bullying and incivility in the workplace.

Understanding the Workplace Bullying Phenomenon

Workplace bullying is a serious epidemic. The impact of this phenomenon affects all workers from the shop floor to the boardroom. (Middleton-May & Zawodskin, 2002). It not only lowers productivity, but also threatens the very root of organizational civility while laying waste to valuable human resources.

The phenomenon of workplace bullying is little understood and is usually ignored. It is usually written off as mere personality conflict, profiling, or prejudice. Few people recognize how abuse proliferates throughout an organization and there are unconscious norms that quiet observers. Unfortunately society is unwilling to recognize the problem and bring the issue to light (Hare & Wyatt, 1997).

Bagshaw (2004), writes that conflicts and disputes are social constructs and can arise from differences in power, opinion, values, interests, needs, communication, and relationship factors such as stereotyping, prejudging, misunderstandings and cultural differences, and etcetera. Conflict in the workplace, addressed as bullying, has come to mean an overbearing, threatening, or forceful person. "Bullying may be further delineated in terms of the frequency and duration of the behavior, the reaction of the target, balance of power between parties, and the interest of the perpetrator" (Hoel, Rayner, & Cooper, 1999, pp. 56-57).

Bullying is very subjective because what one observer may perceive as bullying, another may not. Perceptions are often tainted with our own experiences and assumptions that differ from those of others. This clouds the perception of bullying as harmful and precludes helpful approaches in addressing its causes. Problems in definitions point to a need to move beyond definition to explorations and identification of the strategies related to bullying which, as previously mentioned, may be either direct or indirect. Direct bullying targets the victim, while indirect bullying is the spill-over effect on others in the organization (Rathery, 2005).

According to a 2001 report published under the auspices of the Health and Safety Authority (HSA), bullying could further reasonably be regarded as undermining the individual's right to dignity at work, and may cause problems ranging from stress to serious health problems for the bullied individual as well as lead to low productivity for the organization. According to The Office of the Employee Ombudsman (1999), a key component of bullying is power imbalance. According to Bourant (2001), there are three other key components: One, bullying is defined in terms of its effect on the recipient, not the intention of the bully; two, it has a negative impact on the victim; and three, it is a repeated activity.

Bullying and Harrassment

Bullying is often lumped with harassment, where it loses its meaning. However, workplace bullying and harassment, although a fine line exists between the two, are not the same. Bullying more closely resembles domestic violence in that bullying and domestic violence both involve an addiction to power and they are both centered on controlling others in a detrimental way (Brodie & Brosky, 1976). They involve repeated and persistent attempts by one person to torment, wear down, frustrate, or get a reaction from another.

Employment Services Agencies such as the Human Rights Commission are often reported as bully-friendly. In many instances, the bully simply uses the mediation process to merely polish his act (Olsen, 2008). Harassers usually select their targets because they are representative of a social group. Bullies usually do not select targets for this reason and most commonly their targets are not members of social groups with protected group status.

Workplace Incivility

An interesting similarity is found between workplace bullying and general incivility. General incivility is low-intensity conduct that lacks a clear intent to harm, but nevertheless violates social norms and injures targeted employees (Anderson & Pearson, 1999; Cortina et al., 2001). However, incivility is most similar to harassment in that it is a usually a manifestation of gender and race in the workplace (Cortina, 2008). Laws protecting social groups have largely been ineffective in addressing this covert form of discrimination. A problem with most studies of workplace aggression to date is, they focus almost exclusively on "general conduct" while tending to ignore social categories and antisocial work behavior as often against members of undervalued social groups" (Cortina, 2008). As a result, the modern day workplace is often a scene for "formal discrimination" such as unfair selection decisions (e.g. Brief, Dietz, Cohen, Pugh, & Vaslow, 2000; Davido & Gartern, 2000) versus "interpersonal discrimination, which Hebl, Foster, Mannix, and Davido (2002) define as "nonverbal, paraverbal, and . . . verbal behaviors that occur in social interactions" (p. 816).

According to McConahay (1986) modern racism consists of the following principals:

- Discrimination is a thing of the past because Blacks now have the freedom to compete in the marketplace and to enjoy those things they can afford.
- Blacks are pushing too hard, too fast, and into places where they are not wanted.
- These tactics and demands are unfair.
- Therefore, recent gains are undeserved and the prestige granting institutions of society giving Blacks more attention and the concomitant states than they deserve (1986, 1992, 1993).

These views are seen as empirical fact rather than racist opinion or ideology.

Those holding these views, may publicly condemn racism and identify themselves as non-prejudiced. Their explicit rejection of overt bias combined with implicit antiminority or antifemale beliefs yields subtle, unintentional, and unconscious forms of discrimination (Cortina, 2008).

Modern racists and sexists seek to maintain an egalitarian identity, so as work bullies, they base their disparate conduct on unrelated inadequacies not pertaining to race and gender (Brief et al., 1995, 1997, 2000; James, Brief, Diety, & Cohen, 2001; McConahay, 1986; McConahay & Hough, 1976). Scholars are beginning to realize that future research needs to focus towards newer forms of racism and discrimination, as antiquated beliefs and overt racism become less common (Deitch et al., 2003).

Bullies often perceive themselves as managers. However, according to Field (1996), they do not exhibit management skills. To manage is to "motivate staff, minimize cost, maximize profit, and meet targets. Bullies are primarily interested not in achieving these goals, but are rather interested in their personal self-motivation in promoting feelings of their superiority while undermining the feelings of others.

According to Deeming (1950), managers in western organizations assert a right to control people, a right to objectify people, and a right to deny their autonomy. Such traditional views of management roles enhance bullying in organizations. Drucker (1954), contended that management is the organ of society and expresses the basic beliefs of modern western society.

It expresses the belief in the possibility of controlling livelihood through systematic organization of economic resources. It expresses the belief that economic change can be made into the most powerful engine for human betterment and social justice.

That bullies are perceived by others as well as themselves, as managers, should come to no surprise since management is "the least known and least understood" of our basic institutions. Often those in a business do not understand the proper role of management. The bully with reckless management practices leaves the victim defenseless in a sea of power and imbalances. According to a 1999 report of the International Labor Organization (ILO), physical and emotional violence is one of the most serious problems facing the workplace in the 'new millennium." Their definitions of violence include: "any incident which a person is abused, threatened, or assaulted in circumstances relating to this work. These behaviors could originate from customers and co-workers at any level of the organization. Included in this definition are all forms of harassment, bullying, intimidation, physical threats, assaults, robbery, and other abusing behaviors (Hood, 2004).

However, bullying rarely involves physical violence. It generally involves covert psychological violence. It crosses all boundaries of gender, race, religion, and sexual orientation (Namie, 2003). Heinz Leyman, a German psychiatrist, was first to draw the link between workplace incivilities and psychological assaults. The term "mobbing" was used to describe this phenomenon. The British later adopted the term "workplace bullying (Namie, 2003).

Mobbing begins as an emotional assault on a person identified as a target for disrespectful and harmful behavior. A hostile environment is created for the target with an objective to force the targeted person out of the workplace.

Innuendos, rumors, and public discrediting are often used which may escalate to "abusive and terrorizing" behavior (Lorenz, 1993).

Lorenz (1993), compared mobbing to the behavior of birds. Birds do not physically attack their victim, but surround it with non-physical assaults until the victim has been destroyed. In a similar situation, the target of workplace bullying exists surrounded by attackers. Those not joining the attack fear defending the victim as they may become targets (Namie, 2003).

According to Gary and Ruth Namie (2003), bullying is nearly invisible. As a form of psychological violence, it exists in a covert and gray area which is hard to identify.

Yet most bullying would end if organizations would not tolerate it. One difficulty organizations where bullying exists has, is that the practice of bullying has long been established in its ranks (Hidge, Hoel, & Corey, 2001). Bullying also continues because successful organizations may tend to ignore it.

The Bullying Process

"Bullying is of often viewed as tough management" (Namie & Namie, 2002, p. 3), but it is not tough management, it is a phenomenon that creates chaos in organizations, initiated by someone who knowingly abuses the rights of others to gain control of a situation and/or the individual involved, using persistent intimidation and manipulation techniques to get their way. "Targets may be accidently selected, but usually selection is based on desirable qualities they possess such as competence, networking, and emotional intelligence" (p. 23).

According to the Canadian Safety Council (2000), adult bullies tend to be insecure people like their child schoolyard counterparts. They have poor or no social skills and little empathy. This feeling of insecurity is turned outward and used as a weapon to attack and diminish capable people. Tactics used include:

- The target is subjected to unjustified criticism.
- The bully employs trivial fault-finding

- The target is humiliated, especially in front of others.

- The target is ignored, overruled, isolated, and excluded.

- The target may be set up for failure by setting up unrealistic goals or deadlines, denying necessary information and resources, either overloading the target with work or taking all work away (sometimes replacing proper work with demeaning jobs) or increasing responsibility while removing authority.

The targeted worker receives an unrelenting stream of harm to reduce his/her performance, self-esteem, and value to ultimately terminate his employment. There is also the factor of ". . . repeated aggression with the intention of inflicting pain in whatever form the bully selects" (Randall, 1977, p. 4).

Many targets say that their productivity bottoms out under the stress and eventually they succumb to the physical effects of working in this negative environment (Rossi, 2006). Horsten (1996), suggests the disrespectful behavior produces a toxin that paralyzes its victims, draining energy, initiative, and desire while undermining their physical and psychological well-being. He also points out that subordinates may also be bosses and render some of the same behavior on their bosses as they lament about their bosses. Workplace bullies have been categorized as "controllers" while victims have been categorized as "co-operators," and their values of openness and fair play are viewed as weaknesses by perpetrators (Namie & Namie, 2003).

The bully has at his disposal the ability to destroy and create an organizational climate that is most harmful to people (Namie & Namie, 2002, p. 3). As organizational leadership accepts bullying, an environment of psychological threat is established eventually leading to less corporate productivity with an decrease of individual and group affective commitment (Comer & Vega, 2005).

Leyman (1993) identified five phases of the mobbing or bullying process:

- A conflict or critical incident occurs.
- Aggressive acts and psychological assaults set the mobbing dynamic into motion.
- Management supports these assaults on the victim by extending support to the perpetrator and begins the isolation and expulsion process.
- The victim is labeled as difficult or mentally ill which almost always leads to expulsion or resignation

- The victim may develop posttraumatic stress disorder or psychometric illness.

When bullies sense others observing them, they seek to express justification for their behavior. The target is placed under scrutiny and inquisition. Often, after a few weeks, a trivial incident or minor indiscretion is identified or invented to use as a basis for disciplinary proceedings. Bullies also exhibit a "Jekyll and Hyde" attitude, which enables them to convince management to use the personnel department as a tool to eliminate an employee (Field, 1996).

Often, the victim's personnel records are scanned to gather harmful evidence. A case is often fabricated using words like, "sub-standard work performance," "non-cooperation," "insubordination," and "gross misconduct" (Field, 1996). Feelings of insecurity may abound in the bully and are augmented by management's support. The bully may be untouched by laws, making him immune to prosecution. Field (1996) further suggested that a bully-boss who has followed a non-bully predecessor often dismantles the target's work quickly and with little adversity. The perpetrator may also win the co-operation of co-workers who remain silent to protect their own interests. As a consequence, an environment of hatred and fear engulfs the workplace directed toward the victim who becomes increasingly isolated and criticized.

Additionally, the bully may develop a more comprehensive plan of attack if he or she feels the victim is difficult to subjugate. This plan can only succeed in a bully tolerant organization. At first, it appears to benefit the victim, but actually, it has been designed to intimidate and control. It may include the dual-control method which ploys one person against another while both are unsure or what is happening. Another ploy is the nice-guy intermediary, where bullies employ a nice-guy as an intermediary. This person may be aware of what is happening, but does not want to object for fear of job security.

"Betrayal of Trust" is a tool often used by the bully. The target develops trust in an individual and the individual may even be a best friend. Ultimately this individual hurts the victim through betrayal. Betrayals are often portrayed in multi-bully scenarios.

The new boss forms a coalition with a previous boss to entrap the victim. The victim now asks himself, "Why me?" Issues are not clarified driving the victim into further humiliation until he begins to blame himself with shame and guilt, which leads to further deterioration of the victim's self-confidence and self-esteem.

Victims are trapped by a job, they love, but a position they hate (Field, 1996). They are constantly worried by the threat of job loss, the security of financial dependents, and may be loyal to the needs of the customers, clients and family members. As stress increases, they become more introverted, unable to deduce what is wrong with them.

Eventually victims feel powerless and develop learned helplessness. Their suffering may impact their families as thoughts are consumed by experiences in the workplace.

Some even turn to drugs and alcohol and some have been known to become suicidal. Some families have even been known to suffer breakup due to the stress associated with bullying. Workplaces that are bully tolerant become quite pathological and gripped with fear, with everyone including management being too petrified to hold the bully accountable. The environment in these workplaces have been described as similar to a police state.

Additionally, unconscious norms that are embedded in the culture of the workplace have co-workers believing that they are prohibited from speaking out. These norms are compounded by the norm of silence in society (Chauncery & Wyatt, 1997).

Group norms draw workers into collisions that helps determine how people react. A prerequisite for scapegoating is one must conform to the group norms or becomes an outsider.

The scapegoating may become acute to the point that an individual is targeted and railroaded out of an organization. The bully's hold according to Field (1996) seems to comprise dependency, approval, loss of control, isolation, amoral behavior, and fear. Victims respond to this humiliation by reaching out for acceptance and approval. The victim then looses self-control because the perpetrator becomes the determiner of behavior and the victim sees no outlet from their frustration. The bully will not change his objective despite any grief experienced by the victim or any efforts to improve work performance.

Improving work performance, only makes the bully more determined to destroy the victim, since the victim's ability to perform is usually a reason for his initial selection as a target. In order to disguise, his objective, a bully may actually assist a victim in enhancing performance for a while, but this assistance is short-lived. In the long-term, the bully comes back to demean the victim over his or her performance.

Once a target is eliminated, the hunger for control is not satisfied. The bully begins looking for another target to eliminate and the cycle begins again. Performance declines as a result of persistent harassment and abuse and there are no rewards, only punishment and pain. People learn to avoid the behavior/tack/situations that invoke unfavorable outcomes. The target, is thus, punished for being a good performer. If there are no bad performances, the bully creates them or builds them out of futile mistakes. Financial rewards may enhance or sustain performance for a while, but then have an opposite effect if people are not also rewarded with pleasurable feelings that come from feeling like valued human beings (Field, 1996).

If a target feels isolated from others in the workplace and receives no support from colleagues, experiences may not be shared that may be used as evidence against the bully. In many instances, colleagues may even be warned by the bully to stay away from the victim. The use and spreading of rumors and the writing of statements are also often used by the bully to aid in the endeavor, and to build an environment of hostility against the victim.

Bullies often feel they are immune from persecution because they are seldom summoned to account for their behavior. Many have long standing networks in the organization that assure their positions despite their behavior. In addition from receiving management support, they are usually well liked by others in the workplace. This support is coupled by the subtle fears of those in opposition.

Bullies are not necessarily more capable, professional, wise, or knowledgeable, than the victim, but have the support of the organization. They often lack the "people skills" needed to be fair and objective. Many have reached their position by persuading their superiors that they are the right person for the job, regardless of their ability to do the work (Field, 1996). A considerable amount of time is spent by bullies defending their actions and winning support. They poison the environment of the workplace and eventually, because bullying leads to less efficiency, absenteeism and high staff turnover, lawsuits may result. Unfortunately, in rare cases, violent incidents may occur.

According to Einarsen and Hoel (2001), bullying is either work-related or personal. Examples of work-related bullying would be giving employees unreasonable deadlines or unmanageable workloads, maintaining the employee's tasks exceedingly, or assigning meaningless tasks, perhaps too little or no tasks. Personal bullying includes behavior such as insulting remarks, exclusive teasing, spreading gossip or rumors, persistent criticism, practical jokes, and intimidation. Those events persistently directed towards a targeted individual may cause extreme harm and damage to the individual (Wikkelsen & Einarsen, 2002).

Most people have the ability to cope with workplace bullying. However bullying has long-term consequences both on and off the job. Its persistency may drain the coping resources of the victim (Leyman, 1990 b). Hence, the frequency and duration of bullying may be as important as the actual nature of the behavior involved (Einarsen, 2000 b). Einarsen (1999), framed four stages in the bullying process They are:

- Aggressive behavior
- Bullying
- Stigmatization
- Severe trauma

Targets withdraw for fear of rejection, criticism, and humiliation. In many cases, they withdraw because they are ignored by others when trying to communicate with them, even when they have good ideas and suggestions. The result may be a loss of team spirit and could lead the victim to develop a dependence on alcohol or other substances. This in turn leads to impoverished performance, poor concentration, and failing memory (Field, 1996). The victim eventually is cut off from support in their working environment, escalating the bullying process (Leyman, 1986). The victim may also become helpless with lengthy sick absences and no role left in the workplace. This last stage, (Leyman, 1990b), referred to as 'expulsion' and victims are either forced out of the workplace or leave voluntarily (p. 16). This escalation is a key aspect of the conflict literature (Rubin et al., 1994) and has only recently made its way into research literature.

Role of Organizations in Promoting Bullying

According to Leyman (1996), the workplace is the only remaining working 'battlefield' where people can run into each other without being taken into court. There are no laws prohibiting workplace bullying and unless taken more seriously, more and more people will be psychologically injured. The severity of this phenomenon is far worse than other behavior prohibited by law. Its grueling prevalence indicates a worsening trend affecting all in the workplace, victims and non-victims alike. This practice, however, is not new, but its effect on the health and well-being of those victimized is gradually coming to realization. According to Rossi (2006), "A Canadian survey found that physical violence is usually reported from outside sources while psychological violence is more often reported within the organization." "This is believed to be due to the salient nature of bullying that requires entailed observation to identify it" (Rossi, 2006, p. 7).

Research conducted in the last 2 decades has identified negative organizational climate as leading to psychological stress. This is further upheld by statistics showing job stress in estimated to cost the American Industry $200 to $300 billion annually and the skyrocketing cost of worker compensation claim (Namie, 2002, 2003). Statistics show bullied targets have a 70% chance of losing their jobs, leading to post-traumatic stress disorder (PTSD). The bully destroys not only the victim but also his community and support system (Namie, 2003). At the apex of this destruction is violence that may result from the acute scapegoating that may be characterized by bullying.

PTSD follows acute stress disorder with symptoms that include disorientation, confusion, intense agitation, and dazed detachment and amnesia. The trauma resulting from workplace bullying may be as real to the victim as witnessing a tragic event (Adams, 1992).

Bullying qualifies as trauma because it consists of cumulative assaults on targets, competence, confidence, self-image, and job security as the bully insists on perceiving the individual as a worthless human being. The event is unreal to a competent person who loses competence and self-esteem and an emotional shock is produced for a person who had expected to be treated fairly. Trauma is partly the result of a violation of one's expectations, of idealistic assumption shattered by a cruel reality (Adams, 1992).

Perceptions of the Bully

Escalation of bullying techniques causes replication of the bully's habits throughout the organization, even though the bullying campaign may be based on fuzzy and unspecific information about the target. Often, this unspecific information is supported by authoritarian organizations that have rigid controls. These organizations may not view bullying practices as unacceptable and the practices as normal. There are no rules in the company handbook prohibiting it, and even if there were, in many cases management would not comply with them (Field, 1996). This toxic behavior permeates the culture and climate of an organization that allows bullies to operate unmitigated, and is typically found to be consistent throughout all levels of the organization.

According to Namie (2003), workers in directive, authoritarian organizations are often unsatisfied because their needs are being ignored. Workers are further humiliated as the organization allows those at the "top" prerogative power central, have little interaction and communication with those at the bottom (Namie, 2003). The injustice goes unchallenged for three reasons:

a. People do not see the misuse of power.
b. The belief that working people as well as managers are incapable of supervising themselves and must have "leaders", who are inherently superior.
c. People lack the behavioral knowledge and skills necessary to envision collaborative organizations and make them function.

This perception of line workers as being inferior enhances the process, because it supports the "blame the victim" mentality. Brodsky (1976), states that in order for bullying to be established in a given environment, it must occur within a culture that supports or even rewards this kind of behavior.

Leyman (1996), added that mobbing is widely practiced in government organizations. While these organizations have high job security, there are few objective measures of performance. There is frequent tension between loyalty to the institution and loyalty to the purpose of the organization. Nursing and social service fields display these similar characteristics, which help to explain why bullying is more pronounced in these professions.

Leyman (1996), also asserted that poor conflict management contributes to conflicts, which escalate to bullying because managers or supervisors deny its appearance or may also be participators in the behavior.

Zapf, Knory & Kulla (1996), suggested that conflicts affect information flow and leader-member relationships. They also restrict a worker's opportunity to affect decision-making (Leyman, 1990a). Einarsen (1999) identified two types of bullying and situations needed for bullying to thrive. The first is predatory bullying; the victim accidentally falls into a situation where the predator is demonstrating power or exploiting weaknesses. This type of bullying most often occurs in organizations that have bullying cultural venues. The victim, in their case, may be seen singled out and bullied due to membership in a certain group or be perceived as representative of a group or category of people who are disapproved by the dominant organizational culture. These employees may be bullied merely for showing up for work (Archer, 1999).

Predatory bullying may also be initiated simply because a victim is perceived as an easy target. The source of the stress and frustration is difficult to define, inaccessible, or too powerful or respected to be attacked, and the group may turn its hostility towards a suitable scapegoat (Theylefaces, 1987). These groups develop unrestricted aggression, and hostility prevails, with the bullying often acting as a collective defense mechanism (Bjorkquist, 1992).

Dispute-related bullying occurs as a result of highly escalated interpersonal conflicts (Einarsen, 1999; Laff & Scass, 2001). Although there is a thin line between interpersonal conflicts and bullying, the difference lies in frequency and direction of the aggressor. According to Leyman (1996), it also lies in the ability of both parties to defend themselves in this situation. Although bullies may be peers or even subordinates, bullying usually exists in situations where there is a power imbalance, in such scenarios as with a superior and a line worker. The line worker is in a defenseless position with organizational support favoring the superior who may be the bully.

The social climate at work may escalate into harsh personalized conflict or even office work wars. The objective becomes ultimately to destroy the opponent (Van de Vliet, 1998). Conflict escalates as a signal is sent throughout the organization indicating the organization tailors incivility and rudeness (Namie, 2002, 2003). Management in these organizations has a 'hands-off' attitude until the situation has reached a magnitude of uncontrollable proportions. It is often believed, that once the victim reaches a certain point, he will "explode emotionally" or no longer tolerate the bullying. Emotional explosion is a natural consequence for human beings, as they can only take so much before breaking down. Once this occurs, the victim is blamed for the explosion and actions are immediately taken against him without identifying problems, which were causative of the outburst.

Although others in the organization witnesses the emotional explosion, they usually remain silent, because it may be that they have joined a clique with the bully, or they may fear becoming targets themselves (Riggio, 2011). If the bully has been successful in an approach of divide and conquer, the target could have been easily isolated, and others will not be seen to be supportive.

The Bully-Prone Workplace

According to Namie (2003), there are some proven characteristics of a bully prone workplace. One, they are organizations that that are constantly pressed for "making the numbers". The budget cuts in social service agencies may lead to harshness and create a climate of cutthroat completion and disrespect. Two, they may be organizations in which recruitment, provocativeness, and reward systems form and support an individual's "strengths of personality" or interpersonal aggressiveness, while ignoring emotional intelligence. Problems develop when people are placed in managerial or supervisory positions without accounting for their ability and/or willingness to be objective in evaluating subordinates. Even though superiors or managers may possess high technical skills, and even may be well liked by some persons in the organization, they can easily turn to bullying. Three, organizations with only short-term plans may become bully prone organizations. There is little vision as to where the organization is going and hysteria develops in the work environment, giving rise to climates of distrust and disrespect.

The fourth characteristic is that organizations may become prone to bullying if their interval conduct codes do not clearly identify what is "normally defined" illegal incidents. These incidents are those, which are prohibited by law or by the organization's code of conduct as delineated by the employee handbook. Five, in some bully prone organizations, executives give higher priority to personal friendship than to legitimate interests. The bully may often have the favor of executives and faces no accountability of their actions. Other workers become irritated knowing they will not be promoted regardless of how well they perform over a favorite of management.

Six, bully-prone organizations usually generate feelings of fear among employees. Employees fear losing their jobs because they are insecure in positions where they are constantly being pushed to 'make numbers' and work requirements change constantly, because there is no long range planning.

Ruthless cost cutting and mergers have caused whole layers of management to instantly disappear, affecting those in lower levels of the organization, while those at the top have the options of large salaries, resources, and share (Field,

1996). Leadership therefore clearly sends the message, even if unspoken, that to move higher positions in the organization, you must conform to its gluttonous behavior in response to ever tightening budgets. (Fields, 1996).

Organizational Denial of Bullying

Usually when management is confronted with punishing a bully, it either denies the allegation or lightly punishes the bully. Punishment measures may be counseling or training. Most often, management denies the abuse due to three popular threatened beliefs:

- People operate as independent individuals and are not controlled by group pressure.
- People's behavior is under continuous rational control.
- Workplaces have people's interests at heart (Adams, 1992).

Denial is a defense that only fails when the problem can no longer be denied. It establishes a barricade that helps block the pain arising from situations from beyond control. Entire groups may remain in denial if they are unwilling to change behavior. Norms establish denial in order to prevent change and insure that the values of the group remain intact. If members of the group contest the norms, they face rejection from the group and ultimately may become victims of bullying. Norms are also enforced by the "norm of silence," which prevents members of the group from speaking out about change.

The norm of silence establishes a homeostatic rule that makes discussing problems taboo. Because there is silence, people in the culture will either not hear you, resist you, misunderstand you, or feel attacked as they try to draw their attention to the norms which guarantee that the normative behaviors in the organization will not change (Adams, 1992). These norms do not erase organizational values. Organizations may hold values that contradict practices. Norms, however, are not always negative, as organizations may also have positive norms that support the health of the organization.

The question may arise, "Why do people adopt unfavorable organizational norms?"

One answer is people generally operate best when their behavior is congruent with that of the group and they are not being distracted by internal struggles and anxieties. They, therefore block out those interruptions which may lead to increased elevations of stress.

People also adopt norms psychologically due to dependence or feedback from others, to reinforce positive confirmation of their self-esteem (Adams, 1992).

In adopting organizational norms, several steps are followed:

1. Individual recognizes the need to conform.

2. He begins to see the world through the reality of the new beliefs aided by necessary rationalizations that still are being constructed.

3. The individual believes that the norms are reality while joining other group members in enforcing the norms on each other.

4. People blame themselves for any remaining pain of having to do it "their way," and use norm enforcement (Adams, 1992).

In addition to resorting to denials, organizations seldom resolve conflicts and resort to scapegoating. As a result, the worker may feel that he or she is working in a minefield as management often punishes the worker without due process when it feels undermined or when found to be in error (Namie, 2003).

As co-workers side with the bully, the victim's strong allies, who once stood with him or her, become opponents. Their opposition remains even after the victim has left the organization. The victim is often blamed for their fate, to protect those left behind (Namie, 2003). An irony is Americans love competition. So they grasp the axiom, "winners take all, targets are losers", being lured to the side of the bully while the target is shunned (Adams, 1992).

Preventive Methods at the Primary, Secondary, and Tertiary Levels

According to Adams (1992), "Organizations need to resolve conflicts when they first occur. People need to ask questions such as 'how can this situation be resolved swiftly, legally, and with the least harm to all concerned?" (p. 17). According to cooper et al. (2000), the employer should adopt ways to inform managers and staff of guidelines and codes of ethics to encourage ethical behavior, confidence, in one's professionalism, a climate of tolerance and freedom of attitude, and discourage refusal to collaborate or engagement in improper behavior. The code of silence needs to be broken And the use of mediation and impartial third parties may be considered, although, many consultants feel mediation is not the proper way to deal with cases of workplace bullying.

The rationale for this position is predicated upon the continued belief that abusive practices lead to successful organizations and therefore must be alright. The complaining employee is the suspect-after all what is one individual up against many well qualified and experienced managers? The employee is labeled as a "trouble maker" or senior management claims the troubles are due to personality differences. The complaining employee is seen as expendable, is ignored, and consequently moves on or out (Olsen, 2008).

Rather than first seeking mediation to solve bullying, the organization must first act to protect the complainant. A standard non-victimization clause should be part of any complaint process. If the allegation is found to have substance, the perpetrator should be given directives to change or leave. This process should then be managed as with other kind of hazard.

Workplace bullying should be treated as serious misconduct that seriously harms individuals (Olsen, 2008).

Many complainants report that employment relations services and the Human Rights Commission are bully-friendly. They report having received further abuse and damage by the process of mediation. Many of them become ill prior to the process and are traumatized within the process as well. In many cases, the workplace bully uses mediation to simply polish their act. Human Rights Commissions and the employment relations authorities need to recognize workplace bullying as a serious problem and action should be taken to remove the policy of mediation after the first instance (Olsen, 2008).

Prompt and serious responses are needed to encounter any attacks upon the victim.

In situations where mediation can negotiate a solution, the bully should not be identified, but the mediator should analyze what has happened and then establish the terms of an arrangement in order for the parties to the complaint to continue to work together in an environment of greater mutual respect (Cooper et al., 2001). Health problems should be identified early to help reduce harmful consequences for the victim's psychological and physical as well as other members of the victim's social network and the work environment (Cooper et al. 2001).

Organizations That
Do Not Want to Change

In spite of measures that may be taken by organizations to prevent and alleviate bullying, many will refuse to take these measures. Researchers find that in 1 in 20 work groups is fully supportive of its members and clinical research shows that any work group not fully supportive is at risk for bullying (Cooper et al., 2001).

The Rensis Likert Survey of Organization Data Bank show that less than 1 in 10 US work groups are fully collaborative. The worker is handicapped by a system belonging to management (Cooper et al.). People in the lowest levels of the organization also may resist change. Many feel that management is not to be trusted and the proposed changes will never happen. This is clearly relevant because a collaborative organization, which values its employees, is 75% less likely to condone or tolerate environments which are toxic to employees and the organization, and this includes bullying and all forms of violence in the workplace (Cooper et al., 2001).

A fully tolerant manager, may never propose ending bullying, due to a sense of failure, shame, or inadequacy that makes him feel he has to approve the demands of those in inferior positions, or worse yet, those he feels he has to direct, because they are incapable of directing themselves.

The change, in this case will have to be imposed on the organization from outside and management will have to address the issue. Many will attempt to evade compliance with rules on the books.

This is why it is extremely important for all those in the workplace to be educated about bullying and know its symptoms. Shared knowledge has been called "Collaborative Awareness".

Collaborative group processes may be initiated which are generally more effective than conciliatory services such as the Employee Advisory Program (EAP).

Victims also report that they have not been adequately represented by the EAP. This tool of the organization, was originally established to aid alcoholics. It is not Knowledgeable enough regarding work issues and seldom will go against management. It usually returns the victim to the cycle of abuse with little remedy. In fact, the bully may even use this referral to suggest that the victim, and not the bully has the real problem, adding to the strategy of creating even greater adversity (Cooper et al., 2001).

Mobbing: Emotional Abuse in the Workplace

Mobbing is also a term use to identify workplace bullying. Mobbing in an organization spreads like a cancer, spreading rapidly and attacking "anyone" rather than focusing on specific discrimination based on age, gender, race, creed, nationality, disability or pregnancy using harassing, abusive, and often terrorizing behavior. According to Cooper et al. (2001), it is done intentionally to force a person out of the workplace.

According to Leyman (1993), there are 45 mobbing behaviors in 5 Different categories:

- Impact of self-expression and the way communication happens
- Attacks on one's social relations
- Attacks on your reputation
- Attacks on the quality of one's professional and life situation
- Direct attacks on a person's health

Mobbing has also been called a "syndrome" because like a syndrome, it consists of numerous factors occurring simultaneously with the goal of injuring health. It is a "ganging up" by the leader(s), organization, superiors, co-workers, or subordinates who rally others into systematic and frequent mob-like behavior. The organization may often ignore, condone, and in some cases, even instigate the behavior (Davenport, Schwartz & Elliott, 1999)

There are 3 degrees of mobbing, according to (Davenport et al.,1999).

Each corresponds to successive effects on the mobbed. The degrees were determined by the intensity, duration, and frequency of the mobbing, the psychology of the mobbed individuals, their upbringing, past experience, and general circumstances (Davenport, 1999).

1. 1st degree: Victim manages to resist, escapes at an early stage, or is fully rehabilitated in the same workplace or somewhere else.
2. 2nd degree: Victim cannot resist nor escape immediately, and suffer temporary or prolonged mental/and or physical disability, and has difficulty reentering the workplace.

3. 3rd degree: The affected person is unable to re-enter the workforce. The physical and mental injuries are such that rehabilitation seems unlikely, unless a very specialized treatment protocol is being applied.

Mobbing not only affects one's dignity, integrity, credibility, and professional competence, but one's physical and psychological health. Symptoms of ill-effects include: loss of concentration lessening of performance, and frequent absence due to illness, which impacts the organization and puts the mobbed at fault. The organization ultimately finds grounds to terminate the employee or force resignation.

Mobbing is very problematic under law. It does not fall under current civil rights law and the abuses occur in a gray area. The practice of mobbing often continues unhampered, eliminating those who are not liked to feed the mobber's pleasure and hunger to control or reinforce prejudice (Davenport et al., 1999). When the practice becomes an integral part of the organization's culture, it disappears from the awareness of those in the organization. It is crucial, that mobbing and bullying behaviors be identified immediately to prevent the implantation of this cancer

The Impact of Organizational Culture

Organizational culture is defined as the personality of an organization (McNamara, 1997). When first entering in a company's door, one can make a brief assessment of its culture by noticing the furniture arrangement, how workers are dressed, and what they are talking about. Organizational (a) culture is formed from four components: assumptions, (b) values, (c) norms, and (d) tangible signs. These cohesive elements are shared by members and those not sharing them are regarded as outsiders.

According to Becker and Gear (1960), organizational culture is a set of common understandings around which action is organized. Finding expression in language and whose manners are peculiar to the group. Louis (1980) stated that there are understandings or meanings shared by particular groups that are not shared by outsiders.

Workplace bullying erupts in organizations and spreads rapidly through tacit communication channels. The covert nature helps to conceal and preserve its presence.

Witnesses may understand what is happening, but fear exposing the injustice.

The bully understands the organization's unwillingness to admit to bullying and feels secure in his role due to organizational support.

According to McNamara (1997, 2007), there are four types of cultures:

- Academy Culture-employees are highly skilled and choose a stay with To stay with the organization and work their way up in the ranks. Examples of such organizations include universities, hospitals, large Corporations and etcetera.
- Baseball Team Culture-These include organizations such as investment banks and advertising agencies. They have highly skilled employees who can easily find jobs.
- Club Culture-The military exemplifies this type of culture as well as some law firms. Employees must fit into the culture and seniority is highly valued for promotion.
- Fortress Culture-Employees are uncertain about their future with the organization.

These organizations often undergo massive reorganization. Examples of these types of organizations include savings and loans and large car companies.

In addition to the types of cultures, Schein (1988), identifies three levels of cultures:

They are behavior and artifacts, values and assumptions, and beliefs. Behavior and artifacts are observable and consist of behavior patterns and outward manifestations of culture, which include prerequisites provided to executives, dress codes, level of technology utilized (and where it is utilized), and the physical layout of work spaces.

Values are not directly observable but they are manifested in behavior.

Schein (1988) contended that assumptions and beliefs spring from values and ultimately are taken for granted dropping out of awareness.

The impact of organizational culture on individuals cannot be over instated Culture is everywhere (Koylouiski, Chao, Smith, & Hedland, 1993). Culture effects employee morale, commitment, productivity, physical health, and emotional well-being. Empirical research has produced an impressive array of findings, demonstrating the importance of culture to enhance organizational performance (Cameron & Ettington, 1988; Denison, 1990; Trice & Beuyer, 1993).

Organizational cultures are no longer static as the world has shifted to an information economy. More information has been produced in the last 20 years than was produced in the previous 5,000 years. A weekday edition of the New York Times or the Herald Tribune contains more information than the average person was likely to come across in their lifetime during the 17th century. The total amount of information available to the average person doubles every five years (Chaos & Al, 1993).

This rapid influx in organizational change requires the worker to continuously act to insure productivity. Organizations have the supreme challenge of effectively addressing change while they are often unsure of how to implement change. A survey of corporate executives in six industrialized countries revealed that less than half had achieved their cost-cutting goals through downsizing. Even fewer met operating goals such as improved productivity (Chao et al., 1993).

Another survey found that in downsized companies, employee morale, and trust also suffered due to downsizing.

Companies that engaged in reengineering displayed similar results in another survey (Chao et al., 1993).

A fundamental reason for failures due to downsizing, mergers, and reengineering is the failure to realize the importance of cultural changes. When culture remains constant, the organization will resort to its status quo despite strategic procedures to move forward (Chao et al., 1993). This key component has only been recently realized in promoting organizational change. It is important to realize that organizational culture represents "how things are around here". It reflects the prevailing ideology that people carry inside their minds.

The Role of Leadership

A leader's success is in large measure dependent upon an understanding of organizational culture. Many leaders, when trying to implement new strategies or a strategic plan leading to a new vision, will discover that their strategies were inconsistent with the organization's culture and therefore were not successful.

Leadership is best understood as a moral endeavor. The leader must both articulate a vision and a purpose for followers and simultaneously honor their rights. The leader must exercise power with moral integrity and principles (Whetstone, 2005). An ethical leader promotes and practices good values in spite of pressures to promote and practice bad values. A leader can resist pressures, even with great sacrifice, to compromise good ethics, which depends on the sensitivity of the situation and circumstances. Character is vulnerable to the environment, but it is also a bulwark against the environment. Leaders must therefore, have the ability to safeguard ethical standards despite challenges from the environment (Whetstone, 2005).

Toxic and fear-based cultures such as those produced by bullying, lower ethical concerns by causing leaders and others in the organization to withdraw, build their own "story" of reality, imagine others are out to get them, and react accordingly (Whetstone, 2005).

Leaders must combat the development of fear by creating cultures where all team members can contribute their talents and reach their potential. They need to create a feed-back rich culture, so that everyone is open to feedback and their ideas are valued. Colleagues must learn to work in concert, develop higher level skills, learn from each other, meet performance goals, and turn breakdowns into breakthroughs.

Paine (1994), proposed two strategies in promoting ethical organizations: Integrity strategies and compliance strategies. Integrity strategies involve decision making at every level of the organization with decisions formulated, implemented, and assessed in light of a consensual commitment to ethical concerns. Compliance strategies define the rules of what is acceptable or unacceptable in the organization. However a compliance strategy without ethical perspectives, is of limited value (Martin, 2003). Enron and Arthur Anderson are examples of organizations that had strong compliance departments, yet weak ethical constraints. Eventually this inefficiency led to their collapse.

The leader must establish and maintain trust with ethics and communicate the vision and mission across all sub-cultural boundaries. He or she must serve as a role model because role-modeling helps others internalize the desired values. He or she must help define the culture by rewarding the desired behaviors and shunning undesired behavior.

However, it must be remembered that leaders who promote and/or participate in bullying and intimidation do not provide good inspiration, they only accelerate the decline of the organization.

In summary, organizational culture and leadership are interwoven. Culture defines the role of leadership (Schein, 1985). Leaders embed and reinforce culture (Schein, 1985). If leadership allows bullying to become embodied in the culture and does not combat it, he or she will be tacitly reinforcing the bullying behaviors.

References

Adams, A. (1992). *Bullying at work: how to confront and overcome it.* London: Virago Press.,

Anderson, L. & Pearson, C. (1999). Tit for tat? the spiraling effect of incivility in the workplace. *Academy of Management Review, 24; 452-471.*

32,1051-1056.

Aquino, K., Tripps, T.M., & Bies, R.J. (2001). "How employees respond to personal offense: The effects of blame attribution, victim status, and offender status on revenge and reconciliation in the workplace, *Journal of Applied Psychology, vol. 86 (1), February, pp. 52-49.*

Archer, D. (1999). Exploring bullying culture in the para-military organization, *International Journal of Manpower, 20,1, 2, 94-105.*

Becker, S. and Geer, B (1960). Latent culture: a note on the theory of latent social roles, *Administrative Quarterly, vol 5,2, 304-313.*

Bjorkquist, K. (1992). Sex differences in physical, verbal, and indirect aggression: A review of recent research, *Sex Roles, 30, pp. 177-188.*

Bjorkquist, K. et al (1994). Aggression among university employees, *Aggressive Behavior, (20), 173-84.*

Bourant, R. (2001). Understanding workplace bullying: a practical application of giddens structuration theory, *International Education Journal, no. 4, Educational Research* Conference. 2001 Special issue, http://www.flinders.edu. ar/education/iey

Brief, A.P., Dietz, J. Cohen, R.R., Pugh, S.D., & Vaslow, J.B. 2000. Just doing business: Modern racism and obedience to authority as employment discrimination. *Organizational Behavior and Human Decision Processes, 81:72-97.*

Brodsky,C. (1976). *The harassed worker,* Lexington Books: OC Health & Co., MA; Toronto.

Cameron, K. S. & Ettngton, D.R. (1988). The conceptual foundations of organizational culture, in Smart, J. C.

(Eds), *Higher Education: Handbook of Theory and Research*, Agathon Press, New York: NY, Vol. 4, pp.356-96.

Canada Safety Council (2000). Bullying in the workplace, http://www.safety *council.org/info/Osa/bullies.html*.

Canada Safety Council (2006). *Bullying in the workplace.* [online]. Available: http://www.safety-council.org/info/ OSH/bullies.html.

Chao, G. T. (1993). Complexities in international organizational socialization, *Journal of Personality and Social Psychology, 65, pp. 723-734.*

Chao, G., Koylowski, S., Smith, E., & Hedlund, J. (1993). Organizational downsizing: strategies, Interventions and research implications, *International Review of Industrial and Organizational Psychology, 8, 263-332.*

Chauncery, H. and Wyatt, J. (1997). *Work abuse: How to recognize and survive it,* Schenkman Books.

Cooper, C., & Hoel, H. (2001). Destructive conflict and bullying at work, Manchester School of Management: *University of Manchester Science and Technology, November (2000).*

Cortina, L.M., Magley, V.J., Williams, J.H. and Langhout, R.D. (2001). Incivility in the Workplace: Incidence and impact. *Journal of Occupational Health Psychology,* *6,64-80.*

Davenport, N., Schwartz, R.D. Y Eliott, G.P., (1999, 2002, 2005). *Mobbing: emotional abuse in the American workplace,* Civil Society. Publishing: Amer, Iowa.

Davido, J.F. and Gaertner, S.L. (2000). *Reducing intergroup bias: The common intergroup identity model.* Philadelphia, PA: Psychology Press of Francis & Taylor.

Deitch, A.E., Barsky, A., Bisty, R.M., Brief, A.P., Chan, S., and Bradley, J.C. (2003) Subtle yet significant: The existence and impact of everyday discrimination in the workplace, *Human Relations, 56, 1299-1324.*

Deeming, E. (1950). *Some theory of sampling,* New York, NY: John Wiley & Sons.

Denison, D.R. (1990). *Corporate culture and organizational effectiveness,* New York, NY: John Wiley & Sons.

Diety, J., Robinson, S.L., Folger, R., Baron, R.A., and Schuly, M. (2003). The impact of community violence and an organization's procedural justice climate on workplace aggression. *Academy of Management Journal, 48 (3), pp. 317-326.*

Dovido, J., & Gaertner, S. (1998, 2005). *On the nature of contemporary prejudice: the causes, consequences, and challenges of aversive racism. In J. L.Eberhardt & S.T. Fiske (Eds,). Confronting racism: the problem and the response*: 3-32: Sage: Thousand Oaks, CA.

Dovido, J.F., Hebl, M.R., Foster, J.B., & Mannix, L.M. (2002). Formal and interpersonal discrimination: A field study of bias toward homosexual applicants, *Personality and Social Psychology Bulletin, vol.28, no.6,815-825.*

Drucker, P.F. (1954). *The practice of management*, Harper & Row Publisher, Inc., New York/NY.

Duffy, M.K., Ganster, D.C., & Pagon, M. (2002). Social undermining in the workplace, *Academy of Management Journal, 45, 331-351.*

Einarsen, S. (1999). The nature and causes of bullying at work, *International Journal of Manpower, 20, 16-27.*

Einarsen, S. (2000). Harassment and bullying at work: A review of the Scandinavian approach *Aggression and Violent Behavior. 5,* 379-401.

Einarsen, S. and Hoel, H. (2001). The negative acts questionnaire: Development, validation, and revision of a measure of bullying at work, *Tenth European Conference on Work and Organizational Psychology, Prague.*

Ellis, H. C., Moore, B.A.,Vance, L.J., and Ottaway, S.A. (1997). Depressed mood, task organization, cognitive interference and memory: Irrelevant thoughts predict recall performances, *Journal of Social Behavior and Personality, 12 (2)*, 453-470.

Erez, A., and Porath, C. (2007). Does rudeness really matter? The effects of rudeness on task performance and helpfulness. *Available at papers.ssrn.com/so/3/papers.cfm? abstract-id=986441.*

Field, T. (1996). *Bully in sight, how to predict, resist, challenge and combat workplace bullying,* Success Unlimited; Oxoshire, England.

Hare, C. & Wyatt, J. (1997) *Work abuse: how to recognize and survive it.* Schenkman Books. *International, 58,* p. 4725.

Hebl, M.R., Foster, J.B., Mannix, L.M., Dovido, J.F. (2002). Formal and interpersonal Discrimination: A field of study of bias toward homosexual applicants, *Personality and Social Psychology Bulletin, 28 (6),* 815-825.

Hoel,H. & Cooper, C. (2000), Extracts of destructive conflict and bullying at work of study report compiled for launch of the civil services, *Race Equality Network (September 2001).*

Hoel, H., Rayner, C. & Cooper, C.L. (1999).Workplace bullying, In C. L. Cooper and I. T. Robertson

(Eds),*Organizational Psychology, 14 (pp. 195-229). New York: John Wiley.*

Hoel, H., Cooper, C.L., and Faragher, B. (2001). The experiences of bully in Great Britain: The impact of organizational status. *European Journal of Work and Organizational Psychology, 10(4),443-465.*

Hoel, H., and Cooper, C.L. (2001). *Building a culture of respect managing bullying at work,* CRC Press.

Hood, S. (2004). Workplace bullying. *Canadian Business., 77(18) 887-90.*

James, E., Brief, A. P., Diety, J., and Cohen, R. R. (2001). Prejudice matters: Understanding the reactions of whites to affirmative action programs targeted to benefit blacks, *of Applied Psychology, 86,6, 1120-1126.*

Judge, T.A., Thorsen, C.J., Bono, J.E., and Patton, G.K. (2001). The job satisfaction-

Job performance relationship: A qualitative and quantitative review. *Psychological Bulletin, 127,* 376-407.

Kozlowski, S.W., Chao, G.T., Smith, E.M., and Hedlund, J. (1993). Organizational downsizing: Strategies, interventions, and research implications. *International Review of Industrial and Organizational Psychology: 263-332. New York, NY: John Wiley.*

Kvale, S. (1996). *Interviews: An introduction to qualitative research interviewing,* Thoucsand Oaks,CA:Sage Publications.

Leyman, H. (1990). Mobbing and psychological terror at workplace, *Violence and victims, pp119-126.*

Lorenz, K. (1996). *On aggression,* Deutscher Taschenbach Verlog Gmt H. & Co. KG:Munich.

Louis, M.R. (1980). Surprise and sense-making: What newcomers experience in entering unfamiliar organizational settings. *Administrative Science Quarterly, 25,* 226-251.

Martin, J. (2000). Hidden gendered assumptions in mainstream organizational theory and research, *Journal of Management Inquiry, 9,* pp. 207-216.

McConahay, J. B. (1986) Modern racism, ambivalence, and the modern racism scale. *In J.F. Dovido & S.L. Gaertuer (Eds), Prejudice, Discrimination, and Racism 91-125,*

McConahay, J. B., & Hough, J.C., (1976*).* Symbolic racism, *Journal of Social Issues, 32: 23-45.*

McNamara, C. (1997). Organizational culture, *Authencity Consulting, LLC. Adapted from the Field Guide to Leadership and Supervision.*

McNamara, C., (2007). Basics in internal organizational communication. Free Management Library Website. Retrieved from the world wide web internet on http://managementhely.org/marktng/org.htm

Mikkelsen, E. and Einarsen, S. (2002). Relationships between exposure to bullying at work and psychological and psychosomatic health complaints: The role of state affectivity and generalized self-efficacy. *Scandinavian Journal of Psychology, 43,* 397-405.

Namie,G. & Namie, R., (2000;2003), *The bully at work: what you can do to stop the hurt and reclaim your dignity on the job,* Source Books, INC., Naperville, Ill.

Namie, G. (2003). *Workplace bullying: escalated incivility*; *Inez Business Journal: Nov/Dec.*

Olsen, H. (2008). Mediation is not the way to deal with cases of workplace bullying, *Wave: www.wave.org.172/docs/mediation/html.*

Paice, E. & Firth-Cozens, J. (2003). "Who's a bully then?" BMJ (Clinical Research/ed). 2003;326 (7393):512, http:www.bmj.vom.

Paine, L.S. (1994). Managing organizational integrity, *Harvard Business Review, March-April: 106-107.*

Paine, L.S. (1994). Forging the New Salesman, *(Harvard Business School case studies) Harvard Business School.*

Pearson, C.M. and Porath, C.L. (2005). On the nature, consequences and remedies of Incivility: No time for 'nice?' think again, *Academy of Management Executive, 19*:7-18.

Peyton, P.R. (2003). *Dignity at work, eliminate bullying and create a positive working Environment,* London:England: Routledge, Taylor & Francis Group.

Randall, P. (1997). *Adult bullying, perpetrators and victims,* Routledge; London, NY.

Rathery, G. (2005), Bashing the bully pulpit, *American Society for Training and Development,*

Riggio, R. (2011). Why workplace bullies thrive: The bystander effect! What can be done to stop workplace bullying in cutting edge leadership, *www.psychologytoday. com/blog/ cutting-edge-leadership 2011/01/why-work-place-bullies-thrive-the-bystander effect.*

Rossi, J. (2006). From the bully pulpit, *American Society for Training and Development.*

Rossi, A.M., Quick, J.C., Perreine, P.L. and Santu, S.l. (2006). Stress and quality of working life: Current perspectives in organizational health, Charlotte, NC:AP Information Age Publishing Inc.,

Rubin, J.Z., Pruitt, D.G., and kim, S.H. (1994). *Social conflict: escalation, stalemate, and settlement (2nd ed.)* New York, NY: McGraw-Hill.

Schein, E, H. (1988). Organizational culture, *WP#2088-88, Sloan Management School.*

Thdylefors, S. (1987). Synbockar on exclusions and bullying in worklife, *Stockholm, Sweden: Naturohr Kulton.*

Trice, H.M. & Beyer, J.M. (1993). *The culture of work organizations.* Prentice Hall, Englewood, Cliffs, N.J.

Tyler, T.R., and Blader, S. (2000). *Co-operation in groups: Procedural justice, social identity, and behavioral engagement.* Philadephia, PA: Psychology Press.

Varner, L.J., and Ellis, H.C. (1998). Cognitive activity and psychological arousal: Processes that mediate mood-congruent memory. *Memory and Cognition, 26,* 939-950.

Zapf, D., Knory, C., & Kulla, M. (1996). On the relationship between mobbing factors, and job content, social work environment, and health outcomes, *European Journal of Work and Occupational Psychology, 5 (2),215-237.*

9 781951 886417